# AMAZING ANIMALS OF THE WORLD ①

Volume 2

**Bobolink — Cottonmouth**

GROLIER

an imprint of

◧SCHOLASTIC

Scholastic Library Publishing

www.scholastic.com/librarypublishing

First published 2008 by Grolier, an imprint of Scholastic Inc.

For information address the publisher: Grolier, Scholastic Library Publishing
90 Old Sherman Turnpike
Danbury, CT 06816

Printed and bound in the U.S.A.

Library of Congress Cataloging-in-Publication Data
Amazing animals of the world 1.
v. cm.
Contents: v. 1. Aardvark-bobcat — v. 2. Bobolink-cottonmouth — v. 3. Coyote-fish, Siamese fighting — v. 4. Fisher-hummingbird, ruby-throated — v. 5. Hyena, brown-mantis, praying — v. 6. Marmoset, common-owl, great horned — v. 7. Owl, pygmy-robin, American — v. 8. Sailfin, giant-spider, black widow — v. 9. Spider, garden-turtle, common musk — v. 10. Turtle, green sea-zebrafish.
Includes bibliographical references and index.
ISBN 0-7172-6225-1; 978-0-7172-6225-0 (set : alk. Paper) - ISBN 0-7172-6226-X; 978-0-7172-6226-7 (v. 1 : alk. paper) - ISBN 0-7172-6227-8; 978-0-7172-6227-4 (v. 2 : alk. paper) - ISBN 0-7172-6228-6; 978-0-7172-6228-1 (v. 3 : alk. paper) - ISBN 0-7172-6229-4; 978-7172-6229-8 (v. 4 : alk. paper) - ISBN 0-7172-6230-8; 978-7172-6230-4 (v. 5 : alk. paper) - ISBN 0-7172-6231-6; 978-0-7172-6231-1 (v. 6 : alk. paper) - ISBN 0-7172-6232-4; 978-0-7172-6232-8 (v. 7 : alk. paper) - ISBN 0-7172-6233-2; 978-0-7172-6233-5 (v. 8 : alk. paper) - ISBN 0-7172-6234-0; 978-0-7172-6234-2 (v. 9 : alk. paper) - ISBN 0-7172-6235-9; 978-0-7172-6235-9 (v. 10 : alk. paper)
1. Animals—Encyclopedias, Juvenile. I. Grolier Incorporated. II. Title: Amazing animals of the world one.
QL49.A453 2007
590.3—dc22

2007012982

# About This Set

Amazing Animals of the World 1 brings you pictures of 400 exciting creatures, and important information about how and where they live.

Each page shows just one species, or individual type, of animal. They all fall into seven main categories, or groups, of animals (classes and phylums scientifically) identified on each page with an icon (picture)—amphibians, arthropods, birds, fish, mammals, other invertebrates, and reptiles. Short explanations of what these group names mean, and other terms used commonly in the set, appear in the Glossary.

Scientists use all kinds of groupings to help them sort out the thousands of types of animals that exist today and once wandered the earth (extinct species). Kingdoms, classes, phylums, genus, and species are among the key words here that are also explained in the Glossary.

Where animals live is important to know as well. Each of the species in this set lives in a particular place in the world, which you can see outlined on the map on each page. And in those places, the animals tend to favor a particular habitat—an environment the animal finds suitable for life—with food, shelter, and safety from predators that might eat it. There they also find ways to coexist with other animals in the area that might eat somewhat different food, use different homes, and so on.

Each of the main habitats is named on the page and given an icon, or picture, to help you envision it. The habitat names are further defined in the Glossary.

As well as being part of groups like species, animals fall into other categories that help us understand their lives or behavior. You will find these categories in the Glossary, where you will learn about carnivores, herbivores, and other types of animals.

And there is more information you might want about an animal—its size, diet, where it lives, and how it carries on its species—the way it creates its young. All these facts and more appear in the data boxes at the top of each page.

Finally, the set is arranged alphabetically by the most common name of the species. That puts most beetles, for example, together in a group so you can compare them easily.

But some animals' names are not so common, and they don't appear near others like them. For instance, the chamois is a kind of goat or antelope. To find animals that are similar—or to locate any species—look in the Index at the end of each book in the set. It lists all animals by their various names (you will find the Giant South American River Turtle under Turtle, Giant South American River, and also under its other name—Arrau). And you will find all birds, fish, and so on gathered under their broader groupings.

Similarly, smaller like groups appear in the Set Index as well—butterflies include swallowtails and blues, for example.

# Table of Contents
## Volume 2

# Glossary

**Amphibians**—species usually born from eggs in water or wet places, which change (metamorphose) into land animals. Frogs and salamanders are typical. They breathe through their skin mainly and have no scales.

**Arctic and Antarctic**—icy, cold, dry areas at the ends of the globe that lack trees but are home to small plants that grow in thawed areas (tundra). Penguins and seals are common inhabitants.

**Arthropods**—animals with segmented bodies, hard outer skin, and jointed legs, such as spiders and crabs.

**Birds**—born from eggs, these creatures have wings and often can fly. Eagles, pigeons, and penguins are all birds, though penguins cannot fly through the air.

**Carnivores**—they are animals that eat other animals. Many species do eat each other sometimes, and a few eat dead animals. Lions kill their prey and eat it, while vultures clean up dead bodies of animals.

**Cities, Towns, and Farms**—places where people live and have built or used the land and share it with many species. Sometimes these animals live in human homes or just nearby.

**Class**—part, or division, of a phylum.

**Deserts**—dry, usually warm areas where animals often are more active on cooler nights or near water sources. Owls, scorpions, and jack rabbits are common in American deserts.

**Endangered**—some animals in this set are marked as endangered because it is possible they will become extinct soon.

**Extinct**—these species have died out completely for whatever reason.

**Family**—part of an order.

**Fish**—water animals (aquatic) that typically are born from eggs and breathe through gills. Trout and eels are fish, though whales and dolphins are not (they are mammals).

**Forests and Mountains**—places where evergreen (coniferous) and leaf-shedding (deciduous) trees are common, or that rise in elevation to make cool, separate habitats. Rain forests are different (see below).

**Freshwater**—lakes, rivers, and the like carry fresh water (unlike Oceans and Shores, where the water is salty). Fish and birds abound, as do insects, frogs, and mammals.

**Genus**—part of a family.

**Grasslands**—habitats with few trees and light rainfall. Grasslands often lie between forests and deserts, and they are home to birds, coyotes, antelope, and snakes, as well as many other kinds of animals.

**Herbivores**—these animals eat mainly plants. Typical are hoofed animals (ungulates) that are common on grasslands, such as antelope or deer. Domestic (nonwild) ones are cows and horses.

**Hibernators**—species that live in harsh areas with very cold winters slow down their functions then become inactive or dormant.

**Invertebrates**—animals that lack backbones or internal skeletons. Many, such as insects and shrimp, have hard outer coverings. Clams and worms are also invertebrates.

**Kingdom**—the largest division of species. All living things are classified in one of the five kingdoms: animals, plants, fungi, protists, and monerans.

**Mammals**—these creatures usually bear live young and feed them on milk from the mother. A few lay eggs (monotremes like the platypus) or nurse young in a pouch (marsupials like opossums and kangaroos).

**Migrators**—some species spend different seasons in different places, moving to where more food, warmth, or safety can be found. Birds often do this, sometimes over long distances, but other types of animals also move seasonally, including fish and mammals.

**Oceans and Shores**—seawater is salty, often deep, and huge. In it live many fish, invertebrates, and some mammals, such as whales and dolphins. On the shore, birds and other creatures often gather.

**Order**—part of a class.

**Phylum**—part of a kingdom.

**Rain forests**—here huge trees grow among many other plants helped by the warm, wet environment. Thousands of species of animals also live in these rich habitats.

**Reptiles**—these species have scales, have lungs to breathe, and lay eggs or give birth to live young. Dinosaurs are thought to have been reptiles, while today the class includes turtles, snakes, lizards, and crocodiles.

**Scientific Name**—the genus and species name of a creature in Latin. For instance, *Canis lupus* is the wolf. Scientific names avoid the confusion possible with common names in any one language or across languages.

**Species**—a group of the same type of living thing. Part of an order.

**Subspecies**—a variety but quite similar part of a species.

**Territorial**—many animals mark out and defend a patch of ground as their home area. Birds and mammals may call very small or very large spots their territories.

**Vertebrates**—animals with backbones and skeletons under their skins.

# Bobolink
*Dolichonyx oryzivorus*

**Length:** 6 to 7¾ inches
**Diet:** insects and grain
**Number of Eggs:** 5 to 6
**Home:** *Summer:* central North America;

*Winter:* South America
**Order:** perching birds
**Family:** buntings, finches

 Grasslands

 Birds

Summer
Winter

© JOHN GERLACH / ANIMALS ANIMALS / EARTH SCENES

The bobolink's bubbly mating call once resounded through New England each spring. "Bob-o-lincoln, bob-o-lincoln" is how many people heard the song. They shortened the phrase to give the bird its present name. Sadly, this sweet song is disappearing from the East Coast, along with the meadows and hayfields where the bobolink once bred. The bird's numbers were already declining in the 1900s, when many were shot. Bobolink meat was considered a tasty morsel to be served at fancy dinners.

The bobolink has two very different diets. In the spring and summer, it eats insects and feeds them to its young. But when it flies south for the winter, the bobolink becomes a grain eater. Its changing appetite fits perfectly with the different kinds of food available in its two homes. Now that rice is rarely grown in the southeastern United States, most bobolinks fly all the way to Argentina for the winter—some 5,000 miles!

Most birds mate for life and share in the rearing of their young. But the male bobolink mates with many females, who then raise their chicks by themselves. This would seem to be a hardship for the female, as she has no one to help her guard her nest. Perhaps for this reason, bobolinks form large, crowded flocks after they mate. In these extended families, the females can easily warn one another should danger approach.

# Bonefish
*Albula vulpes*

**Length:** up to 3½ feet
**Weight:** up to 18 pounds
**Diet:** crustaceans, mussels, and worms
**Method of Reproduction:** egg layer

**Home:** New Jersey south to southern Brazil, and all tropical waters
**Order:** bonefishes and relatives
**Family:** bananafishes, bonefishes

 Oceans and Shores

 Fish

© WILLIAM BOYCE / CORBIS

This cigar-shaped fish is a native of warm tropical waters. But it also roams up the northeastern coast of the United States. It earns its name because of its many small, thin bones. They are nearly impossible to pick out of the fish's flesh.

The bonefish is a popular sport fish because it is a challenge to catch. It is a fast and unpredictable swimmer. Even the best fishermen have difficulty catching it. When it is finally hooked, the bonefish tries hard to get away. Reeling in the line is difficult. This strong, agile fish can twist and fight furiously for hours.

But the bonefish does more than avoid fishermen and other sea predators. It hunts for mussels and worms along the sandy seafloor. It stirs them up by swishing its tail in the sand. The bonefish chews its food rather slowly. It grinds the meat down with many small, blunt teeth.

A baby bonefish is called a larva. It grows into an adult in a strange and fascinating way. When it is born, the fish looks like a tiny eel. It does not develop fins until its body is about 2 inches long. Then the young bonefish actually begins to shrink. When it is back down to 1 inch in length, it takes on the shape of an adult bonefish. Once this change is complete, the fish begins to grow again. It eventually reaches a mature size of about 3 feet.

# Masked Booby
## *Sula dactylatra*

**Length:** 32 to 36 inches
**Wingspan:** 5 feet
**Weight:** about 4 pounds
**Diet:** fish and squid
**Number of Eggs:** 2

**Home:** tropical oceans around the world
**Order:** auks, herons, and relatives
**Family:** boobies

Oceans and Shores

Birds

© WOLFGANG KAEHLER / CORBIS

There are six species of booby. During their first year, the young of all species look virtually alike. They all have brown feathers speckled in white. The masked booby is named for the bluish gray "mask" of skin on its face and upper neck. Its plumage is mainly white, with a border of black feathers on each wing and a black, diamond-shaped tail. Generally males have a bright yellow beak. The beak of the female is dull green. Both sexes have yellow legs.

Masked boobies fly over all the world's tropical seas. Occasionally storms will blow one as far north as the Carolinas on the East Coast or as far as southern California on the West Coast. Like all boobies, the masked species can soar for hours or even days on its long, pointed wings. When a booby spies food in the ocean, it plunges headfirst into the water. It also catches the occasional flying fish that jumps above the surface.

Masked boobies breed throughout the year in scattered colonies on small islands and rocky seashores. The female usually lays two eggs. But the firstborn chick nearly always kills its younger sibling.

The word *booby* means a foolish person. Sailors once named the boobies for their "foolish" trustfulness. The birds will usually allow people to approach and catch them.

# Red-footed Booby
*Sula sula*

**Length:** 26 to 30 inches
**Weight:** 2 to 8 pounds
**Diet:** squid and fish
**Number of Eggs:** 1
**Home:** tropical waters of the Atlantic, Pacific, and Indian oceans

**Order:** auks, herons, and relatives
**Family:** boobies

Oceans and Shores

Birds

© ARTHUR MORRIS / CORBIS

The red-footed booby, a seabird with very long wings, is the smallest of all the world's boobies and is also the friendliest. It frolics around boats and ships, circling and landing on their decks. Sailors have found they can catch a visiting booby quite easily because it cannot take off from the flat surface of a ship. This clumsiness may be why the bird has a reputation for being stupid.

Red-footed boobies are most active at dusk and will even hunt for food in the moonlight, flying above the tropical waters of the Atlantic, Pacific, and Indian oceans. Their streamlined bodies enable them to dive efficiently for the fish and squid that make up their daily diet. When it is time to sleep, they return to their island homes, where they live in large colonies. The booby builds a nest high in a tree, where humans and other predators cannot easily reach it. To further ensure the chick's survival, the female booby concentrates all her energy into laying one very large egg each year. This pale blue-green egg is filled with more than the usual amount of nutrients. The extra food enables the developing chick to remain in its egg for a full month and a half. When it finally pecks its way out, the newborn booby is already quite large and strong and is thus more likely to survive. The booby chick will begin flying in three to four months and grow to adulthood in two to three years. If it manages to stay clear of predators and other dangers, it can live to the ripe old age of 20.

# Bufflehead
*Bucephala albeola*

**Length:** 13 to 15 inches
**Diet:** shellfish, aquatic insects, and fish
**Number of Eggs:** 6 to 14
**Home:** North America

**Order:** ducks, geese, swans, waterfowl
**Family:** ducks, geese, and swans

  Freshwater

Birds

© DARREL GULIN / CORBIS

The bufflehead is a small duck that flies rapidly. The males are called drakes. They have a white patch on the back of the head. The females have a white patch below and behind the eye. Both sexes have a puffy head set on a puffy body. They also have distinctive white wing patches. These are easily seen when the duck flies. During the winter, they are found along the coastal regions of North America. Buffleheads feed on small aquatic animals without backbones. Occasionally they eat fish. They are magnificent fliers.

Buffleheads begin breeding when they are two years old. Pairs form before the ducks arrive at the breeding grounds. Buffleheads do not build nests. Instead they use tree holes left by other birds. A bird will use the same hole year after year. The female usually lays a clutch of nine eggs in the hole. She then lines the hole with down feathers. The male defends the territory during breeding. He continues to do so through the laying period and part of the incubation. Curiously, he usually has flown off by the time the eggs hatch. This event often occurs at night.

The average bufflehead has a life span of seven years. Buffleheads are the smallest hunted waterfowl in North America. They are not afraid of hunters. And they readily return to the exact spot from which they were flushed only minutes earlier.

# Bullfrog
## *Rana catesbeiana*

**Length:** 8 inches
**Weight:** 1 pound
**Diet:** ants, bugs, flies, and worms
**Method of Reproduction:** egg layer

**Home:** eastern and southern North America
**Order:** frogs and toads
**Family:** true frogs

Freshwater

Amphibians

© JOE MCDONALD / CORBIS

The bullfrog's loud call is often heard at night. At this time of day large groups sing in chorus. The bullfrog is the largest of the American frogs. And the females are larger than the males. Bullfrogs live in colonies in or near bodies of still water. They are very territorial animals. A male will spend weeks facing another male in a sort of ritual fight. They stand on their hind legs and embrace. In winter, they hibernate, burrowing into mud at the bottom of ponds.

Bullfrogs react to moving objects. So they are very dependent on their sense of sight and smell. They are fond of insects and snails. But they will also feed on their own young. Frog larvae feed on plant matter.

Bullfrogs mate in the spring. The male makes a characteristic sound to attract females. The female lays up to 20,000 eggs. Each is enclosed in a jellylike sac. After a few hours, depending on the water temperature, the eggs hatch into tadpoles. It can take the tadpole one to three years to complete metamorphosis. Metamorphosis is a marked change in the form or shape of an animal. Adults are typically green with dark spots.

The bullfrog's enemies include snakes, birds, and humans. The frog is a classic animal to use in classroom dissection experiments. Bullfrog legs are a favorite gourmet dish. Chemical pesticides and now-banned DDT have wiped out entire frog populations in some ponds.

# African Bullfrog
*Pyxicephalus adspersus*

**Length:** 3¼ to 8 inches
**Diet:** frogs, rodents, and birds
**Number of Eggs:** 3,000 to 4,000

**Home:** central, eastern, and southern Africa
**Order:** frogs and toads
**Family:** true frogs

 Grasslands

Amphibians

© JOE MCDONALD / CORBIS

Frogs and toads are hungry predators. They usually eat anything that fits in their mouths. For the African bullfrog, that's a lot! This animal's huge mouth is attached to a fat, round belly. American bullfrogs are happy to eat flies. But their African cousins gobble up large frogs, rodents, and even birds. A favorite is the plump African wattle.

The bullfrog is not a clever hunter. Its instinct tells it to snap only when it sees a prey animal move. However, bullfrogs are very patient. Few small animals can resist the urge to run. But once its prey so much as twitches, the bullfrog pounces. And it swallows its meal in one gulp.

Most frogs and toads are eaten by many animals. Such is not the case with the African bullfrog. When bothered, it can swell its body like a balloon. This makes it a very difficult bite to swallow. The African bullfrog is also aggressive and quick to bite.

This bullfrog is unusual because it lives in hot, dry places. Amphibians usually stay in or near water. This keeps their soft skin moist. The bullfrog does not want to dry out under the strong African sun. So it digs deep in the ground to avoid this. It shovels dirt with the sharp, horny bumps on its back legs. African bullfrogs leave their burrows at only two different times. They come out at night to hunt. And they come out in the rainy season to lay eggs.

# American Bumblebee
*Bombus pennsylvanicus*

**Length:** ½ to 1 inch
**Diet:** clover and flowers
**Method of Reproduction:** egg layer
**Home:** United States, southern Canada, and northern Mexico

**Order:** ants, bees, wasps
**Family:** bumble bees, honey bees, stingless bees

 Cities, Towns, and Farms

 Arthropods

© FRITZ RAUSCHENBACH / ZEFA / CORBIS

Bumblebees produce honey. But they produce less honey than true honeybees do. Bumblebees are usually found in open grasslands. Adult bees have black, hairy bodies with yellow, orange, or red markings. The legs of female bumblebees have stiff hairs, called "pollen baskets." They use them to collect pollen from flowers.

Bumblebees have unique elongated mouthparts that allow them to pollinate red clover. No other bee can do this. Bumblebees are stinging insects and are easily irritated.

All bumblebees except the queen die in autumn. The queen hibernates until spring.

She then selects a nest to begin a colony. She secretes wax to form a cup-shaped cell and stocks it with pollen. She lays about eight eggs in it and seals the cup with wax. When the queen bee isn't gathering pollen, she is "brooding"—warming the larvae cells with her body. In 3 to 5 days, she makes a hole in the wall of the cell and feeds nectar to the larvae. After about 7 days, the larvae hatch. The resulting grubs are white, legless, and hairless. Within about 12 days they develop into hairless worker bees. The workers take over the chores of the growing hive. The queen is busy laying eggs. A colony may grow as large as 2,000 bees. Worker bees live only a few weeks.

# Monarch Butterfly
*Danaus plexippus*

**Wingspan:** 2½ to 4 inches

**Diet:** milkweed (caterpillars); nectar (adults)

**Method of Reproduction:** egg layer

**Home:** North America, the Philippines, Indonesia, Hawaii, and Australia

**Order:** butterflies, moths

**Family:** admirals, angelwings, brush-footed butterflies, and relatives

 Grasslands

 Arthropods

© DAN GURAVICH / CORBIS

During the summer, North American monarch butterflies live in the northern United States and southern Canada. In the fall, they fly south in large groups. During their trip, other groups join them. Soon there are thousands of butterflies in flight. At night, monarch butterflies stop to rest in trees. Sometimes a tree can seem to change into a giant "flower," alive and colorful. These butterflies spend the winter in California or central Mexico. They sometimes cover 2,000 miles. In the spring, the monarchs head north again. Their flight is slow. And they spread out over the countryside. Females lay their eggs during the journey. Caterpillars turn into butterflies. Then they fly north. Most, but not all, reach Canada. They are the children or grandchildren of the butterflies that left Canada the previous fall.

Monarch caterpillars are ringed with bands of white, yellow, and black. They have two pairs of long black threads. These threads are both in the front and in the back of their bodies. When they are upset, they move their antennae violently. The bright colors of the caterpillar and butterfly warn predators to stay away. Caterpillars eat milkweed plants. These are poisonous to other animals. The milkweed poison stays in the insect's body and helps protect it.

Until recently, monarchs lived only in North America. During the last 120 years, they have spread. They now live on islands in the Pacific and Indian oceans. They are also common in Australia.

# Common Buzzard
*Buteo buteo*

**Length:** 18 to 22 inches
**Wingspan:** 40 to 51 inches
**Weight:** 19 to 42 ounces
**Diet:** rodents and other small mammals, birds, frogs, snakes, lizards, insects, and worms

**Number of Eggs:** 2 or 3
**Home:** Europe and Asia
**Order:** daytime birds of prey
**Family:** eagles, hawks

Forests and Mountains

Birds

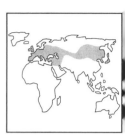

© CHRIS HELLIER / CORBIS

The call of the common buzzard is like the call of another fierce hunter—the domestic cat. The name buzzard, in fact, comes from an old German phrase meaning "meowing eagle."

This bird is common in Europe and Asia. But you won't find more than two in any one place. Each mated pair keeps a territory of 1 or 2 square miles. Parents-to-be usually build their nest in a tree near a field or a forest clearing. The female lays her eggs at the beginning of May. Both parents take turns sitting on the nest until the eggs hatch. This occurs about a month after they're laid.

The common buzzard beats its wings awkwardly when it flies. But it can gracefully glide and soar on the power of the wind. Then it holds its large wings motionless like the sails of a ship. The buzzard seldom catches other birds in flight. It mainly eats chipmunks, mice, voles, and other rodents. How does the buzzard hunt these small animals? It searches the ground from a perch high in a tree or from the air. Once it spots its prey, the buzzard swoops down. It snatches the creature in its strong claws. But the buzzard uses more than its keen sight to hunt. It also uses sound. It listens for the loud call of the cicada. This is a large, tasty insect. Or it may stand on the ground in the evening and listen for the whistle of a chipmunk. These creatures make a delicious meal for an alert buzzard.

# Dwarf Caiman
*Paleosuchus palpebrosus*

**Length:** about 4½ feet
**Diet:** fish, crayfish, frogs, insects, and small birds and mammals
**Number of Eggs:** 20 or 30

**Home:** northern and central South America
**Order:** crocodiles, caimans, and relatives
**Family:** alligators, caimans

 Rain Forests

Reptiles

© JOE MCDONALD / CORBIS

The dwarf caiman is one of the world's smallest crocodilians, an order of animals that includes alligators and crocodiles. Yet, this petite brown-eyed alligator deserves respect. When cornered, a dwarf caiman can deliver a nasty wound with a quick snap of its large, tooth-studded mouth.

The dwarf caiman wears the toughest armor of any species in the caiman family. The horny scales on its body are reinforced on the belly and back by bony plates. The armor can deflect the attack of any natural predator. However, this is little protection against the rifles used by hunters, who kill these creatures in great numbers.

The caiman's strong armor may have developed as protection from the sharp rocks and river debris in the fast-flowing jungle streams of South America. As it rides the rapids over stony riverbeds, the dwarf caiman is often violently tossed about in the shallow water.

Like other alligators and caimans, this species has been hunted for its hide, as well as for the pet trade. In the past two decades, hunters harvested a particularly large number of caimans. Laws now forbid the capture of endangered alligators, but the dwarf caiman is not on the endangered list. Biologists are concerned that the creature may be harmed both by overhunting and by the destruction of its jungle habitat.

# Arabian Camel
*Camelus dromedarius*

**Length:** 7 to 11 feet
**Weight:** 1,000 to 1,450 pounds
**Diet:** herbivorous
**Number of Young:** 1

**Home:** Arabia and North Africa
**Order:** even-toed hoofed mammals
**Family:** camels and relatives

Deserts

Mammals

© FIRST / ZEFA / CORBIS

There are two kinds of camels. The Arabian camel, or dromedary, has one hump. The Bactrian camel of Asia has two humps. Other than the giraffe, the Arabian camel is the tallest land animal. The camel is adapted for life in the desert. Its nose can hold moisture from the air it breathes. Its famous hump stores fat. This allows the camel to survive for days without eating or drinking. When it has no water or food, its body turns the fat into energy and water. A camel can lose up to ⅓ of its weight between meals. But it can drink up to 15 gallons of water in less than ten minutes. In this way it regains its body weight and good health.

During mating season, the Arabian camel becomes nervous and aggressive. Females give birth between February and May, 11 months after mating. The female has a single baby that's covered with a thick, woolly coat. At birth, the baby's eyes are open and it already has a tiny hump.

Today, there are no Arabian camels in the wild. Originally from Arabia, they were tamed and brought to North Africa and Southeast Asia. Camels are used as race animals or to carry loads. They are strong and can travel about 2½ miles per hour for 12 hours in a row. And they can do this while carrying a 300-pound load. People who live in the Arabian and Sahara deserts depend on this animal. They eat camel meat and drink camel milk. They also make clothes from the camel's skin and wool.

# Bactrian Camel
## *Camelus bactrianus*

**Length:** 7 to 11 feet
**Height:** 6 to 8 feet
**Weight:** 1,000 to 1,500 pounds
**Diet:** grasses, leaves, and
  bushes

**Number of Young:** 1
**Home:** Mongolia
**Order:** even-toed hoofed
  mammals
**Family:** camels and relatives

 Deserts

 Mammals

© GEORGE HOLTON / PHOTO RESEARCHERS

? Endangered Animals

There are two different kinds of camels. And people often get them confused. The Arabian camel has only one hump. The Bactrian camel has two. The Bactrian camel is also heavier. And it has a longer and thicker coat. All Arabian camels are now tamed. But some Bactrian camels still live in the wild in the Gobi Desert. This is located between southwest Mongolia and northwest China. There were many wild camels until 1920. Now they are endangered.

Two thousand years ago, travelers rode on Bactrian camels to carry goods and supplies across the plains of Asia. This camel can carry a load of more than 450 pounds. It can travel 20 to 25 miles a day on high, dry plateaus. It can walk along mountaintops more than 10,000 feet high. A Bactrian camel can outrun a horse over long distances. The camel can run for several hours without stopping. In the summer, it can easily survive for two or three days without food and water. In winter, it can live without food and water for up to a week.

In the wild, the Bactrian camel lives in small groups. It looks for grazing grounds in the desert of Central Asia. Grasses, leaves, and bushes make up its daily food. The mating season begins in February. The female carries the single young for 13 months. The baby camel is born in March of the following year.

# White-Throated Capuchin
*Cebus capucinus*

**Length:** 12 to 16 inches; tail: 24 inches
**Diet:** leaves, fruits, small animals

**Number of Young:** 1
**Home:** Central America
**Order:** primates
**Family:** New World monkeys

 Rain Forests

 Mammals

© WOLFGANG KAEHLER / CORBIS

Like most other monkeys, capuchins have a tail that can grasp things, and they use it to pick up objects. Their tail is longer than their body but is not as flexible as those of some other American monkeys. Capuchins are highly intelligent. They are common in zoos and are often kept as pets. Sometimes they are trained to be performers.

Capuchins of several species are found throughout Latin America and in the tropical forests from southern Mexico to northern Argentina. They owe their name to the appearance of some species that have a black "skullcap" (*capuce* in French) on the white hair on their heads. There are some 30 species of capuchin-like monkeys, as well as 4 kinds of capuchins. These monkeys usually live in trees. They do not go down to the ground if they can avoid it, as they prefer high forest trees. They live in groups of a few dozen monkeys. They have well-defined territories, although some territories may overlap. Each community travels on permanent "roads" from one tree to another in single file.

Capuchins have a varied diet. They feed on fruits, nuts, and leaves. They also eat butterflies that they trap in flight and other insects that they find by pulling bark from trees. They raid nests and can even catch birds. Their enemies are birds of prey that eat monkeys, such as the harpy eagle.

18

# Caracal
*Caracal caracal*

**Length of the Body:** 25 to 33 inches
**Length of the Tail:** 8 to 13 inches
**Weight:** 18 to 30 pounds
**Diet:** small mammals and birds

**Number of Young:** 2 to 5
**Home:** dry areas of Africa and southern Asia
**Order:** carnivores
**Family:** cats

 Grasslands

 Mammals

© NIGEL J. DENNIS / PHOTO RESEARCHERS

The caracal, also called the desert lynx, is a born hunter. Like all cats, it moves very quietly until it gets close to its intended victim. Then, in a split second, the creature completes a perfect sneak attack. The caracal is an able jumper, too. It can even stalk a bird from the ground, leap into the air, and capture the bird in midflight! In its search for food, the caracal has the added advantage of camouflage. Its short tan or brown fur blends into the desert surroundings. This "hides" the creature from rabbits, grouse, pheasants, and other prey.

The caracal has many adaptations that make it a great hunter. Its long legs end in wide paws. Some caracals have hair pads on the bottom of their paws. These pads help the creature move across sand. This cat has excellent sight, and its hearing is enhanced by long, pointed ears. Powerful neck and jaw muscles help the caracal grab and kill prey. And sharp teeth stab and do great damage with ease. Despite all these adaptations, the caracal is a favorite prey of leopards, hyenas, and people. Farmers dislike the caracal because it kills lambs and other farm animals.

The female caracal gives birth to her kittens in a hollow tree or an underground den. The kittens weigh less than a pound at birth. The mother nurses the young cats for about four months. During this time she gradually teaches them how to hunt and survive on their own.

# Cardinal
*Cardinalis cardinalis*

**Length:** 8 to 9 inches
**Weight:** 1¼ to 2 ounces
**Diet:** seeds, insects, and fruit
**Number of Eggs:** 2 to 4
**Home:** southern Canada, eastern and southwestern United States, and Mexico

**Order:** perching birds
**Family:** buntings, finches

 Cities, Towns, and Farms

 Birds

© ROYALTY-FREE / CORBIS

A bird sitting in a garden bush whistles "Who-it? who-it? who-it?" The bird is among the easiest of all birds to recognize. It is a male cardinal. He is all red except for a small black patch around his red bill. His mate, sitting nearby, is brown. She has a red bill and some red on her wings and tail. Both birds have a crest of feathers on the top of the head. The red bill is thick and strong. It is used to crush seeds, which are the main food of cardinals. Cardinals also eat berries and insects, including potato beetles and other pests that destroy crops.

Cardinals are songbirds. "Who-it? who-it?" is one of many different songs they sing. Each song is made up of a series of loud, clear whistles. Cardinals do not migrate. They live in the same area throughout the year. Even on a snowy winter day, people can hear cardinals singing.

Female cardinals build cup-shaped nests in bushes and small trees. The nest is made of grasses, bark, roots, and other plant matter. The female lays her eggs in the nest. Then she sits on them until they hatch. Both parents care for the young birds while they are in the nest. Later, after the young leave the nest, only the father cares for them. The mother is busy building a new nest in which to lay more eggs. Cardinals may have as many as three sets of offspring in a single year.

# Sand Cat
*Felis margarita*

**Length of the Body:** 16 to 18 inches
**Length of the Tail:** 9 to 12 inches
**Diet:** lizards, birds, and small rodents

**Number of Young:** 2 to 4
**Home:** from the Sahara and Arabian deserts east to Pakistan
**Order:** carnivores
**Family:** cats

 Deserts

 Mammals

© EFITAL PHOTOGRAPHY / ANIMALS ANIMALS / EARTH SCENES

? Endangered Animals

At first glance the sand cat looks like an ordinary tabby. It's no bigger than a large house cat and has short yellowish red fur. The resemblance is no coincidence. The sand cat is closely related to the African wildcat, *Felis silvestris libyca*. It is believed to be the ancestor of all domestic cats.

Like pet tabbies, the sand cat has a distinct pattern of dark stripes through its fur. In the wild, these markings help camouflage the sand cat against desert rocks and sand. The sand cat is distinguished by its broad head and the wide space between its ears. Its feet are equipped with thick cushions of hair that help it run across deep sand without sinking.

Because this cat is very rare and very shy, scientists know little about it. Like other desert cats, sand cats likely dig burrows in soft sand dunes. The den is a place of refuge from the cold desert night, as well as from the midday heat. Sand cats probably hunt in the early morning and after dusk, when temperatures are moderate.

These creatures have been spotted in places as far apart as Western Sahara, Israel, and Pakistan. Those living in Pakistan are officially endangered. For all we know, all sand cats may be in danger of extinction. On the hopeful side, these felines may survive precisely because they are so careful to avoid humans.

# Woolly Bear Caterpillar
*Isia isabella*

**Length of the Caterpillar:**
about 1½ inches
**Wingspan of the Adult:** about
2 inches
**Diet of the Caterpillar:** mainly
weeds; some crops

**Method of Reproduction:** egg
layer
**Home:** North America
**Order:** butterflies, moths
**Family:** footman moths, tiger
moths

Cities, Towns,
and Farms

Arthropods

The woolly bear caterpillar is a colorful part of American folklore. This bristly caterpillar has black and brown stripes. It's often seen in autumn. It crawls around, searching for cubbyholes where it can spend the winter. Have you ever heard the expression "hurrying like a caterpillar in the fall"? It refers to this animal's busy autumn activity.

Woolly bear caterpillars have also been used to forecast the weather. It is said that the wider the brown band around the woolly bear's middle, the milder the winter. In truth, this band grows wider as the caterpillar matures. So the woolly bear's brown band tells you its age. If the band is especially wide in autumn, it may suggest that the *previous* winter ended early.

Woolly bear caterpillars sleep through the winter. Their favorite places to rest are under bark, logs, stones, boards, and even sidewalks. In spring, they awaken just long enough to eat a snack of tender weeds. Each woolly bear then builds a cocoon out of its own body bristles and a few strands of silk. In about two weeks, an Isabella tiger moth emerges from the cocoon. Its wings are tawny-yellow or orange-brown spotted in black. Many people have never seen this animal in its adult stage. This is because the Isabella is active only at night. Sometime in spring or summer, the Isabellas lay their eggs. These eggs will hatch into the fall's new crop of woolly bears.

# House Centipede
*Scutigera coleoptrata*

**Length:** 1 inch
**Top Speed:** 17 inches per second
**Diet:** insects
**Method of Reproduction:** egg layer

**Home:** Europe
**Order:** long-legged centipedes
**Family:** long-legged centipedes

 Cities, Towns, and Farms

 Arthropods

© DOMINIQUE DELINO / BIOS / PETER ARNOLD, INC.

There are many kinds of centipedes in the world. But *Scutigera coleoptrata* is special in several respects. For starters, this species is one of the fastest. Its long legs make it a good runner. Second, *Scutigera* is more agile than other centipedes. Most important, *Scutigera* centipedes have compound eyes. These allow them to clearly see their surroundings—and possible prey. Other species of centipedes have primitive eyes that perceive only light.

Using their speed and good vision, *Scutigera* centipedes can even catch flies in mid-flight! They catch them with a special pair of poison claws just behind their head. These fanglike claws contain venom that paralyzes and kills their prey. Like all centipedes, *Scutigera* avoids bright light. It is most active at night. It is found in dry places, although it prefers a damp and dark environment. It often hides under rocks, leaves, or fallen logs.

Female *Scutigera* centipedes lay their eggs one at a time. They carry them around on special claws at the end of their body. When the eggs hatch, the young centipedes have four pairs of legs. As they grow, they shed their skin from time to time. During the first six sheddings, or molts, the centipedes grow new legs. Adult *Scutigera* centipedes have 15 pairs of legs. They have the fewest legs of any centipede species.

# Arctic Char
*Salvelinus alpinus*

**Length:** up to 38 inches
**Weight:** up to 27 pounds
**Diet:** small fish, mollusks, and insect larvae
**Method of Reproduction:** egg layer

**Home:** northern areas of North America, Europe, and Asia
**Order:** salmons
**Family:** trouts and salmons

 Freshwater

 Fish

© H. BERTHOULE / JACANA / PHOTO RESEARCHERS

The back and sides of Arctic char are green all year. They're also speckled with large pink spots. Then, as breeding season approaches, its belly turns from a silvery white color to a vibrant red. The male becomes especially colorful at this time.

The Arctic char lives in chilly northern waters. In the southern parts of its range, the char is found in deep lakes. In Arctic areas, the char is a migratory fish. This means that these Arctic char spend most of their adult lives in the sea. But they return to a freshwater river to breed, usually in the fall. Once a breeding site is chosen, the male defends his territory. His mate uses her strong tail to dig a hollow nest in the riverbed gravel. The female deposits her eggs in the nest. The male releases sperm that fertilizes them. Afterward the female sweeps gravel back over the eggs with her tail. The adult char remain in the river through the winter. They return to the ocean in the spring.

Arctic char differ greatly in appearance and behavior. The lake-dwelling varieties are different colors and sizes than their migratory cousins. Some char may never grow more than 8 inches long. Others may be longer than 3 feet! In some places, char prefer to swim in groups. In others, they are solitary. But all char are known for their tasty flesh. Many animals like to make Arctic char part of their diet.

# Cheetah
*Acinonyx jubatus*

**Length:** 4 feet
**Weight:** 100 to 130 pounds
**Diet:** antelope and ostriches
**Number of Young:** 2 to 5

**Home:** Africa
**Order:** carnivores
**Family:** cats

  Grasslands

 Mammals

© TOM BRAKEFIELD / CORBIS

Endangered Animals

The cheetah looks more like a dog than a cat. It has long legs, paws with claws that don't retract, and a small head. These are doglike features—but the cheetah is definitely a member of the cat family, just like lions and tigers.

The cheetah is well known for its speed. This helps it capture gazelles and other antelope. People have used the cheetah's hunting talents since ancient times. Egyptian pharaohs, Russian princes, Mongolian emperors—all had cheetahs in their royal hunts. Unlike some cats, the cheetah creeps very slowly. It stays close to its prey before speeding up to pounce. It is a sprinter, not a long-distance runner. So it becomes discouraged quickly if its prey succeeds in taking the lead.

The cheetah leads a somewhat solitary life. But it does have a social life beyond mating. It usually hunts alone. But groups often organize to hunt together.

The female gives birth three months after mating. The young weigh only 9 to 10 ounces at birth. The parents form a lasting pair. And the male is an attentive father. In spite of this, the death rate of the young is high. Half of them die in the first eight months. Many of them are devoured by lions, hyenas, or leopards.

In the past, the cheetah lived in non-wooded areas of Africa, western Asia, and India. The African species is endangered. But it is holding on, thanks to the creation of reserves.

# King Cheetah
*Acinonyx rex*

**Length of the Body:** 5 feet
**Length of the Tail:** 2½ feet
**Weight:** 120 to 150 pounds
**Diet:** gazelles, impalas, hares, and other small mammals

**Number of Young:** 2 to 8
**Home:** Zimbabwe
**Order:** carnivores
**Family:** cats

 Grasslands

 Mammals

© TOM BRAKEFIELD / CORBIS

Endangered Animals

The cheetah is the fastest animal on Earth, and the grandest of all cheetahs is *Acinonyx rex*, which means the "king" of cheetahs. This species was first described in the 1920s. Hunters returning from safaris in what is now Zimbabwe told of a cheetah unlike any other. While the fur of other cheetahs was short and rough, this newly discovered cheetah had long, soft, luxuriant hair. And while other cheetahs were covered with spots, the king cheetah had many dark bars. The skins of these rare cheetahs became priceless. Only 13 king cheetahs have ever been sighted. These sleek, long-legged cats have not done well since humans began interfering with their lives. They have been hunted for their beautiful fur and captured for pets.

King cheetahs must work very hard for a living. They race after their prey, starting from 70 to 100 yards away. The cheetah is fast. It can go from zero to 45 miles per hour in two seconds. At its speediest, it can reach 70 miles per hour!

All this running means that the cheetah cannot go long without food. A mother feeding her cubs must catch a gazelle or other animal nearly every day. Even solitary cheetahs must eat two or three times a week. The king cheetah will become extinct if people overhunt the animals it needs for food. Fortunately, many African nations are creating wildlife preserves where the king cheetah and its prey can live undisturbed.

# Chimpanzee
*Pan troglodytes*

**Length:** 3 to 4¼ feet
**Weight:** 100 to 175 pounds
**Diet:** mostly fruits, insects, leaves, and seeds, but some meat

**Number of Young:** 1
**Home:** west and central Africa
**Order:** primates
**Family:** great apes

 Rain Forests

 Mammals

© TOM BRAKEFIELD / CORBIS

The chimpanzee is the animal most closely related to humans. It is so intelligent that it makes and uses tools in its daily life. It takes the side branches and leaves off tree limbs to make a stick that will fit into an ants' nest. When the chimpanzee removes the stick, it is covered with insects. The chimpanzee then licks the stick, as you might lick a popsicle!

Chimpanzees live in tropical Africa. They are found in savannas or in forests—sometimes up to an altitude of 10,000 feet. At daybreak, as soon as they wake up, they begin to eat fruits, leaves, and insects. Now and then, they kill young antelope, small baboons, or even other chimpanzees for food. After eating for a few hours, they rest. They eat again in the afternoon. At nightfall, they make a nest in a tree for the night. The nest is made of branches and leaves shaped into a sleeping platform. It may be 30 feet off the ground.

Chimpanzees live in groups of up to 120. All the members of the group have a specific place. This place depends on their size, age, and family relationship. A younger male can be more important than an older male if his mother has a higher position in the community. But males are not very aggressive, and fights are rarely violent.

# Pygmy Chimpanzee
*Pan paniscus*

**Length:** 2½ to 3 feet
**Weight:** 100 pounds (male); 75 pounds (female)
**Diet:** mainly fruits; also other plant matter, insects, and earthworms

**Number of Young:** 1
**Home:** central Africa
**Order:** primates
**Family:** great apes

Rain Forests

Mammals

© KARL AMMANN / CORBIS

The pygmy chimpanzee has earned a reputation as the Tarzan of the animal world. This creature performs breathtaking acrobatic stunts, leaping from tree to tree without ever losing its grip. With equal agility the pygmy chimpanzee scurries across vines suspended high above the jungle floor. In this way the chimp can visit the other members of its community— sometimes as many as 120—who live in the same area. Unexpected visitors are always welcome within the community. In fact, greetings usually include much hugging, kissing, and stroking of one another.

Visits between pygmy chimpanzees are very chatty affairs as well. Frequently the chimps groom one another, picking dirt and insects out of each other's fur. This behavior keeps the animals clean while building strong bonds of love and friendship.

When mealtime rolls around, the pygmy-chimpanzee community breaks up into small groups called troops. Each troop heads off on its own path into the jungle in search of some tasty tidbits. Even the smallest babies accompany the troops on their food forays. A pygmy-chimpanzee baby is completely dependent on its mother for the first two years of life. At first, it clings tightly to its mother's belly. As it grows a bit older, it rides astride its mother's back, much the way a person rides a horse. Either in the troop or at home in the community, the mother lavishes much attention on her young.

# Chinchilla
*Chinchilla lanigera*

**Length:** 10 to 14 inches
**Length of the Tail:** 7 inches
**Weight:** 1 pound
**Diet:** plant matter

**Number of Young:** up to 6
**Home:** Chile and Bolivia
**Order:** rodents
**Family:** chinchillas, viscachas

Forests and Mountains

Mammals

Endangered Animals

© BIOS / PETER ARNOLD, INC.

Chinchillas live high on the rocky Andes Mountains of South America. These rodents are agile. They move quickly from one rock ledge to another. At one time, colonies of 100 or more chinchillas were common in the Andes. Today wild chinchillas are very rare. People overhunted the animals, killing them for their beautiful, silky fur. This fur has more hairs per square inch than that of any other animal. Chinchillas are raised on fur farms around the world. However, farm-raised chinchillas have been specially bred. They are not genetically identical to wild chinchillas.

Even though it gets very cold in their mountain habitat during the winter, chinchillas do not hibernate. They are active throughout the year. They are particularly active at night, when they search for food. They eat almost any kind of plant matter they can find among the mountain rocks. They rarely drink water. All the water they need comes from dew on the plants they eat. During a meal, they squat on their haunches and hold the food in their front paws.

A female chinchilla gives birth to one, two, or three litters each year. A litter contains from one to six babies. At birth the babies are well developed. They have a full coat of fur and large, open eyes. The mother chinchilla is very protective of her babies. Chinchillas live for about 10 years in the wild and up to 20 years in captivity.

# Seventeen-year Cicada
*Magicicada septendecim*

**Length:** 1 to 2 inches
**Diet:** sap from trees and shrubs
**Method of Reproduction:** egg layer
**Number of Eggs:** 400 to 600

**Home:** northeastern United States
**Order:** true bugs, hoppers, aphids, and relatives
**Family:** cicadas

Forests and Mountains

Arthropods

© DOUG WECHSLER / ANIMALS ANIMALS / EARTH SCENES

The seventeen-year cicada is more often heard than seen. That's because the insect lives in trees, often by the thousands. On a hot summer day, these insects make a loud buzzing noise. It can be almost deafening. The male cicada makes the noise by using special drumlike membranes on his abdomen. The sound attracts a female, and they mate. Afterward, the female lays her eggs in slits that she's created on a twig or small branch. The cycle from egg to adult is the longest in the insect world.

In six to seven weeks, the eggs hatch into young, wingless cicadas. These are called nymphs. The nymphs drop to the surface. Then they either enter cracks in the ground or burrow themselves into the soil. There

they draw juice and sap from the roots of trees and shrubs. Their specialized mouthparts help them do this. Thousands may feed on the roots of a single tree without causing the tree any harm. The nymphs remain underground until they mature. This period can last from 13 to 17 years. Then a full-grown nymph emerges. It immediately crawls up a tree or stem and firmly attaches itself to it. Soon the insect sheds its skin. This process is called molting. The discarded skin often clings to the tree or stem surface for many months. The adult cicada is a large blackish insect. It often has green markings. The next day the adult flies off. But the cicada's adulthood is brief. It lasts only 30 to 40 days. It is then that the cicada begins buzzing.

# Atlantic Razor Clam
*Ensis directus*

**Length:** up to 10 inches
**Height:** 1¾ inches
**Diet:** microscopic organisms
**Method of Reproduction:** egg layer

**Home:** coastal waters of eastern North America
**Order:** clams, cockles, and relatives
**Family:** razor shells

  Oceans and Shores

Other Invertebrates

© ANDREW J. MARTINEZ / PHOTO RESEARCHERS

The Atlantic razor clam often leaves a calling card—a long, thin shell. It is found on the beaches of eastern North America. The shell has an opening at each end. It is divided into two equal parts called valves. Strong muscles hold the valves together.

Atlantic razor clams live on the ocean floor. They prefer bays and quiet coastal waters. They move easily along the ocean bottom. They move by contracting the two valves. They also contract a large, muscular "foot." When a razor clam senses danger, it quickly goes to the ocean bottom. Razor clams spend most of their time buried in sand or sandy mud.

A razor clam uses its powerful foot to burrow. The foot changes shape, depending on the clam's needs. For digging, the foot is thin. Once the razor clam is buried, the foot swells up and holds the clam. This makes it hard for a predator to pull the clam out of its burrow.

The foot is at the lower end of the long shell. At the upper end are two tubes. These are called siphons. The siphons go up to the surface of the sand. Water enters the razor clam through one siphon. Cells in the clam's body remove food and oxygen from the water. The second siphon then pushes the water back out into the ocean. If it senses danger, the clam pulls the siphons into the shell.

# Giant Clam
*Tridacna gigas*

**Length:** 3 feet or more
**Weight:** 500 pounds or more
**Diet:** plankton
**Method of Reproduction:** egg layer

**Home:** Indo-Pacific Ocean
**Order:** clams, cockles, and relatives
**Family:** giant clams

 Oceans and Shores

Other Invertebrates

© STEPHEN FRINK / CORBIS

The giant clam is the largest bivalve in the world. Bivalve means that its shell is divided into two parts, or valves. The valves open when the clam eats and rests. The giant clam has been called a human trap. But it is not. In movies it is sometimes shown closing its shell on a diver's leg. But giant clams avoid divers and other large animals. They eat microscopic food called plankton. They filter this food from the water.

Giant clams get food in another way, too. Tiny one-celled organisms live in the lining of the giant clam's shell. These are called algae. Algae, like plants, make food from sunlight. The giant clam provides a safe home for algae. They won't be eaten by passing fish. In return the algae provide food for the clam. Scientists discovered this unusual relationship. They noticed that giant clams usually point their open "mouth" toward the water's surface. They do this to let in sunlight for the algae.

Giant clams live in the warm seas of the Indian and Pacific oceans. Hopefully, they will remain there, thanks to an agreement by many nations. Most governments do not allow giant clams to be brought into their countries for sale.

# Soft-Shelled Clam
*Mya arenaria*

**Length:** about 4 inches
**Width:** about 2½ inches
**Diet:** microbes, organic waste, and small invertebrates
**Method of Reproduction:** egg layer

**Home:** coastlands of North America and Europe
**Order:** soft-shelled clams, piddocks
**Family:** soft-shelled clams

 Oceans and Shores

 Other Invertebrates

As its name suggests, the soft-shelled clam breaks very easily. As a result, beaches on both sides of the Atlantic Ocean are often covered with the crushed white shells of this common clam. Soft-shelled clams can also be found in the Pacific Ocean around San Francisco Bay. The clams probably arrived in the bay in 1874, hidden inside a shipment of eastern oysters. People found the soft-shelled clams to be a delicious gourmet food that can be baked, fried, steamed, or eaten raw.

The soft-shelled clam prefers living in the soft mud under shallow coastal waters. It settles in when it is young and tiny. As it grows, it slowly works itself deeper into the mud, until it reaches a depth of about 15 inches. However, once dug up, the adult soft-shell cannot rebury itself.

The soft-shelled clam breathes and eats through a siphon, or tube. The siphon extends from the clam's soft body, inside its shell, and up to the surface of the mud. As the clam sucks water in through the siphon, it filters out bits of food. It also removes oxygen that is dissolved in the water. Some clams have a second siphon for squirting out their waste. But the soft-shelled clam's main siphon does double duty. The siphon has yet another use at breeding time. Male and female soft-shells blow their sperm and eggs out through their siphons, turning the water into a milky soup.

# Asian Cobra
*Naja naja*

**Length:** usually 4 to 5 feet
**Diet:** rodents, frogs, toads, birds, and eggs
**Number of Eggs:** usually 12 to 24

**Home:** from western Asia to the Philippines and Taiwan
**Order:** scaled reptiles
**Family:** cobras, coral snakes

 Grasslands

 Reptiles

© TONY CROCETTA / PETER ARNOLD, INC.

People in Indian markets often gather to watch a man playing a flute. The man is a snake charmer. As he plays, a cobra rises out of a nearby basket. The snake sways back and forth. It seems to move to the rhythm of the music. But the snake is deaf. It doesn't hear the music. It is just following the man's swaying movements.

Asian cobras live in forests, grassy fields, and rice paddies. When the cobra is excited or scared, the skin on its neck expands into a hood. It raises the front third of its body to an upright position. And it hisses loudly. This behavior is supposed to frighten an enemy. If the enemy doesn't leave, the cobra strikes. Using its fangs, it bites and injects a poison, or venom, into the victim.

The cobra also kills prey this way. Some Asian cobras can even spit venom by pointing their head upward and aiming for the eyes. One drop of cobra venom in the eye of a mouse can kill the mouse. A drop in the eye of a person can cause blindness.

Snake charmers are careful not to be harmed by their cobras. They stay out of the snakes' striking distance. And they work with the snakes during the day. Cobras do not see well in daylight, so it is harder for them to strike. Some charmers take medicine that protects them from cobra poison. Others use cobras that have had their fangs removed.

# Cockatiel
*Nymphicus hollandicus*

**Length:** up to 12 inches
**Diet:** fruits and nuts
**Method of Reproduction:** egg layer

**Number of eggs:** 4 to 7
**Home:** Australia
**Order:** parrots and relatives
**Family:** cockatoos, lories

 Forests and Mountains

 Birds

© ERIC AND DAVID HOSKING / CORBIS

Cockatiels are noisy birds in the wild. This trait makes them clever pets. They can quickly learn to talk. But cockatiels don't seem to understand what they are saying. They just repeat what they hear. The cockatiel is chatty, good natured, and beautiful. It has been a popular pet for more than 300 years. Some have lived 100 years in captivity.

In the wild, cockatiels spend their time in small groups. They hunt for seeds on the ground. They look for fruit and berries in the trees. Cockatiels mate and lay eggs between August and December. The exact time of the year depends on the local conditions. One factor is the amount of rain. Cockatiel nests are usually in small tree holes or in crevices between rocks. The parents take turns sitting on the nests. This keeps the eggs warm. The chicks hatch about three weeks after the eggs are laid. The parents feed the chicks food that has already been chewed and partly digested. In this way they are like many other birds.

There are more than 300 species of parrots. Eighteen of these, including the cockatiel, are called cockatoos. All cockatoos have a crest of feathers on their head. They can move it up and down. The birds display their beautiful crests when they are frightened. Other animals sometimes look to the crest as a red flag of warning. When they see it, trouble is likely nearby.

# Sulphur-Crested Cockatoo
## *Cacatua galerita*

**Length:** 18 to 20 inches
**Diet:** vegetarian
**Number of Eggs:** 2 to 4
**Home:** Australia, New Guinea, and New Zealand

**Order:** parrots and relatives
**Family:** cockatoos, lories

 Forests and Mountains

 Birds

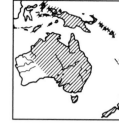

© CAROLYN A. MCKEONE / PHOTO RESEARCHERS

Throughout the year, trees of the Australian tropical forest seem to be covered with large white flowers. But if you look carefully, you will notice that these "flowers" have a very beautiful bright sulfur-yellow crest on the top of their heads. Also, they fly and make sounds. In fact, they are not flowers but very noisy sulfur-crested cockatoos.

The sulfur-crested cockatoo lives in large groups of several thousand birds in forest areas of medium-sized mountains. In flight, this magnificent bird shows its wingspan of more than 3 feet. Besides the sulfur-yellow crest, the cockatoo has a small yellow spot on its cheeks, wings, and tail.

This bird nests in a natural hollow in a tree or in a rock crevice. It doesn't really make a nest but puts wood chips and dry grasses at the bottom of the hole. The female lays two to four white eggs on this bed and sits on them for a month. Both parents feed their young with food they digest for it first.

The cockatoo eats large amounts of grain, which it peels with its enormous beak while holding the stalks between the talons on its feet. It also eats fruits, grasses, and even flowers. During a meal on the ground, the noisy cockatoo is very careful. A few of its flock wait in neighboring trees to act as guards. The guards screech if an enemy approaches. The birds on the ground stop eating and fly up to safer places in trees.

# American Cockroach
*Periplaneta americana*

**Length:** 2 inches or more
**Diet:** garbage, human food, and dead insects
**Method of Reproduction:** egg layer
**Home:** native of Africa; introduced widely

**Order:** cockroaches, termites, mantids
**Family:** American cockroaches, oriental cockroaches

 Cities, Towns, and Farms

 Arthropods

© DONALD SPECKER / ANIMALS ANIMALS / EARTH SCENES

The newspaper headline said "American roach takes top prize." More than 5,000 cockroaches were entered in a contest in Malaysia. The largest was 2.24 inches long. It was an American cockroach. Despite its name, this insect probably came from Africa. Some scientists believe it arrived in the Americas on slave ships. Today it is found almost everywhere. It has hitched rides on ships, airplanes, and other vehicles.

American cockroaches live in warm indoor places. They need a steady supply of food and water. They avoid light. These creatures prefer basements and sewers. Because of this they are often called water bugs. Their flat bodies can squeeze into cracks and other tiny places. They use their long, strong legs to run to hiding places when disturbed. They do not have very good eyesight. To learn about their surroundings, American cockroaches depend on their long, thin antennae. These contain many sensory organs.

Several species are household pests. The German cockroach is very common in the United States. The Asian cockroach is a particular nuisance because it is attracted to light. It was first seen in the United States in Florida in 1985. It is an excellent flier that is as happy outdoors as in. It quickly began to move northward.

# Queen Conch
*Strombus gigas*

**Length of the Shell:** 12 inches
**Width of the Shell:** 8 inches
**Weight:** up to 5 pounds
**Diet:** mainly algae and plant debris
**Method of Reproduction:** egg layer

**Home:** coastal waters from Florida to Brazil
**Order:** slipper shells and relatives
**Family:** true conchs, tibias, and relatives

 Oceans and Shores

Other Invertebrates

© STEPHEN FRINK / CORBIS

The queen conch is a queen-sized snail in a queen-sized shell. This creature lives on sandy and grassy ocean bottoms in warm, shallow water. In order to move from place to place, the conch pushes the clawlike structure on the back of its foot into the sand. It uses this appendage as an anchor—much as a pole-vaulter uses a pole. The conch then vaults, or leaps, over the sand. As it does, its shell flops from side to side.

As the queen conch moves about, its head and large foot extend out of the shell. When it senses danger, it draws its head and foot completely into the safety of the shell. The conch shell looks like a cone-shaped spiral. The smallest whorl, or spiral, is at the tip of the shell. It is the oldest. The largest whorl ends in the opening. The outside of the shell is rough and yellowish. The inside is glossy and rosy pink in color. Under the pink layer is a layer of white. The queen conch shell is prized by divers and souvenir hunters alike.

Fish, crustaceans, and other snails prey on young queen conchs. Loggerhead turtles eat the adults. But the most common predators are people. They eat conch flesh and collect conch shells. The shells are often cut to make jewelry called cameos. As a result, queen conchs are not as common as they once were.

# Andean Condor
*Vultur gryphus*

**Length of the Body:** 3 to 3½ feet
**Length of the Tail:** 13 to 15 inches
**Wingspan:** 9 to 10 feet
**Weight:** 20 to 26 pounds

**Diet:** carcasses and bird eggs
**Number of Eggs:** 1 or 2
**Home:** South America
**Order:** daytime birds of prey
**Family:** American vultures

 Forests and Mountains

 Birds

? Endangered Animals

© LIOR RUBIN / PETER ARNOLD, INC.

The Andean condor is the largest bird of prey in the world. It is easily recognized by the shiny-black feathers on its body and its white collar of fluffy neck feathers. On its head is an odd crest of bright red skin. The male's crest is very large, while the female's is a little smaller.

Once they have bred, two Andean condors will remain together for life. They nest on high, rocky cliffs, mainly in the Andes Mountains. Every other year the female lays one or two eggs. The eggs are pale yellow with small brown spots. Both parents take turns warming the eggs for nearly two months. After hatching, the condor chicks remain in the nest for almost half a year! Even after learning to fly, the young condors stay with their parents for another six months. Together the condor family soars through the sky at amazing heights—up to 19,000 feet! From high above they can spot dead animals lying on the ground miles away. Andean condors that live near the ocean also raid large seabird colonies, where they steal eggs.

Once the Andean condor was once widespread. It is now in danger of extinction. Like its cousin, the endangered California condor, this South American bird has been cruelly hunted. Many ranchers believe that these large birds of prey kill livestock. But that does not seem to be true. The condors are further threatened by the destruction of their natural habitat.

# California Condor
*Gymnogyps californianus*

**Length:** 4 feet
**Wingspan:** up to 9½ feet
**Diet:** carrion
**Number of Eggs:** 1 every other year

**Home:** southern California
**Order:** daytime birds of prey
**Family:** American vultures

Forests and Mountains

Birds

?

Endangered Animals

© JEFF APOIAN / PHOTO RESEARCHERS

The California condor's wings span 9½ feet. It is the largest bird of prey in North America. It is also the heaviest. It can weigh up to 30 pounds. Unfortunately, this beautiful bird holds another record. But it is a sad one. It is the bird of prey most likely to disappear. In 1850, there were condors all along the coast of California and Oregon. But 100 years later, there were just 60 of them left. They have been protected by law since then. But by 1978 there were only 27 of them. In 1987, the last 3 wild specimens were captured for a breeding program. This program has been successful. And the number of condors in captivity is growing slowly. Perhaps some can be reintroduced in the wild soon.

In the wild, this bird builds its nest in areas between 1,600 and 6,500 feet high. Every two years, the female lays one egg at the foot of a cliff. After the egg hatches, both parents feed the baby. The young condor stays in the nest for five months. The parents fly for up to eight hours looking for food. And they may travel more than 30 miles from the nest. At five years of age, the condor gets its feathers. But it must wait another one to two years to mate. The condor has a very long development cycle. This is a challenge for those who are trying to save the bird.

# Copperhead
*Agkistrodon contortrix*

**Length:** 22 to 53 inches
**Diet:** rodents, large insects, birds, and amphibians
**Method of Reproduction:** live bearer

**Number of Young:** 8 to 12
**Home:** central to eastern United States
**Order:** scaled reptiles
**Family:** pit vipers, vipers

 Forests and Mountains

 Reptiles

© ZIG LESZCZYNSKI / ANIMALS ANIMALS / EARTH SCENES

Many people fear the copperhead snake for its poisonous bite. It is true that copperheads account for the largest number of reported snakebites in the United States. But it is also true that their venom is rather weak. Only rarely does a human die from it. Copperheads actually help humans. They capture, kill, and eat an enormous number of mice and other rodents each year.

The skin of the copperhead has a striking color. It is orange with red-brown zigzag bands. This allows the snake to blend—or disappear—into its surroundings. Copperheads dwell on the ground. They prefer to live near swamps, rocky areas,

ditches, and wooded hillsides. Females bear 8 to 12 live young in the late summer or fall. The young snakes have yellow-tipped tails. They twitch them to lure prey. Copperheads spend the winter in groups that often include rattlesnakes.

The copperhead has a special structure called a "pit." It is located between the nostril and the eye. The pit acts as a sensory organ. With it the snake can detect small changes in temperature. It allows the copperhead to "sense" prey. Then, using the prey's body heat, it follows its path. It does this long after the prey has passed from sight.

**41**

# Brain Coral
*Diploria strigosa*

**Width:** up to 26 feet
**Diet:** plankton
**Methods of Reproduction:**
   sexually and asexually

**Home:** Caribbean Sea
**Order:** stony corals
**Family:** brain corals, rose
   corals, star corals

 Oceans and Shores

 Other Invertebrates

© LAWSON WOOD / CORBIS

True to its name, the brain coral resembles a human brain. It is shaped like a dome. And it is covered with many folds and ridges. Like all large corals, the brain coral is actually made up of many small animals. These are fused together and live as a colony.

You may have seen the brain coral in tourist shops. Its unusual shape makes it a popular souvenir. But its popularity is a problem. Coral reefs around the world are endangered. Brain corals themselves are not in danger of extinction. But the reefs where they grow are being destroyed. Pollution, boat traffic, and snorkelers are to blame. Many of them break off coral to sell or keep as trinkets. In 1985, in response to this problem, many countries made it illegal to bring in coral of any kind. The United States and Canada were two such nations. There are two good ways to see brain corals. One is to visit an aquarium. The other is to snorkel around a reef—*carefully*. They may look like hard rocks, but corals are easily damaged and killed.

In nature the brain coral is greenish brown. It gets this color from microscopic algae. These are plants that live in the coral's tissue. The brain coral and the algae have a symbiotic relationship. This means that one helps the other to survive. The algae provide food to the coral. In return, the coral provides minerals and a safe home to the algae.

# Large Flower Coral
*Mussa angulosa*

**Height of the Colony:** 24 inches
**Width of the Colony:** 36 inches
**Diet:** microscopic organisms
**Methods of Reproduction:** sexually and asexually

**Home:** coral reefs in the Bahamas and West Indies
**Order:** stony corals
**Family:** cactus corals

 Oceans and Shores

 Other Invertebrates

© CARLETON RAY / PHOTO RESEARCHERS

The beautiful large flower coral is actually a colony composed of many tiny coral animals. The size of the colony increases when the animals reproduce by budding. In this process a group of cells, called a bud, forms on the side of a large flower coral. The bud enlarges until it becomes a new animal.

Each coral animal secretes a hard, stony skeleton of limestone (calcium carbonate) around itself. Gradually the skeletons of neighboring animals become cemented to one another in one mass. When the animals die, the skeletons remain. Young coral animals build their skeleton on top of the empty skeletons, and the colony becomes bigger and bigger. The skeletons are sharp and spiny. A careless diver who brushes against a large flower coral can get a nasty scrape.

Large flower corals have thick branches packed so closely together that the colonies are usually rounded and look like solid boulders. The corals occur in various colors, including blueish purple, pink, greenish brown, and yellow. They are one of many kinds of corals found in reefs in the Caribbean Sea.

New flower corals form when coral animals reproduce sexually by means of eggs and sperm. The fertilized eggs develop into larvae, which move through the water until they find a hard surface on which to live.

# Cottonmouth
*Agkistrodon piscivorus*

**Length:** 30 to 48 inches
**Diet:** fish, frogs, snakes, and other small animals
**Method of Reproduction:** live-bearer

**Home:** southeastern United States
**Order:** scaled reptiles
**Family:** pit vipers, vipers

 Freshwater

Reptiles

© JOE MCDONALD / CORBIS

The cottonmouth is a big, heavy, and very shy snake. It avoids enemies whenever possible. And that includes people. When disturbed, it escapes by slipping into the water. It dives out of sight or swims away with its head just above the surface. But sometimes it cannot escape. Then the cottonmouth shakes the tip of its tail and faces its enemy. It tilts its head upward and opens its mouth wide. It exposes the white inside. It is this white lining that gives the snake its common name.

Cottonmouths are not usually far from water. They live in swamps, marshes, ponds, streams, rice fields, and ditches. They often sun themselves at the water's edge or on floating logs. In the northern part of their range, they may hibernate in rocky ledges during the winter. They often do this in groups. And they frequently share their dens with rattlesnakes.

Cottonmouths are poisonous. They have long, hollow fangs. These are used to deliver their poison, or venom. At rest, the fangs are folded against the roof of the mouth. When a cottonmouth bites a fish, frog, or other prey, it injects its fangs into the victim. Then it releases the harmful venom. A cottonmouth does not chew its prey. Instead, it opens its mouth very wide, and it slowly swallows the creature whole. If the prey is large, it may take a week or more to digest.